Maple,
The Syrup-Sneezing Tree

by Naveed Mardi

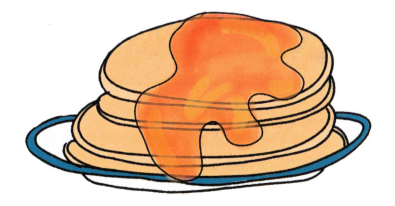

For my mom, who told me I would make a great P.E. teacher. I said I don't see that happening. But here we are-she pretty much called it.

Early in the morning, loud dozers and machines woke Adam up.

He followed his nose downstairs to the smell of pancakes.
Adam loved two things most of all: pancakes and maple syrup.

He sat down, only to discover he was out of maple syrup.

"Sorry! I didn't mean to sneeze on you."
"Don't be sorry! This is amazing!" Adam gobbled down his maple-covered pancakes.
"When I get scared, I sneeze syrup."
"That's gross but... delicious!" said Adam.

CHUGGA CHUGGA BOOF!
The dozers outside were so loud,
Adam and the tree began talking louder.
"My friends call me Maple, and the trees and I need your help! We're all scared right now!"

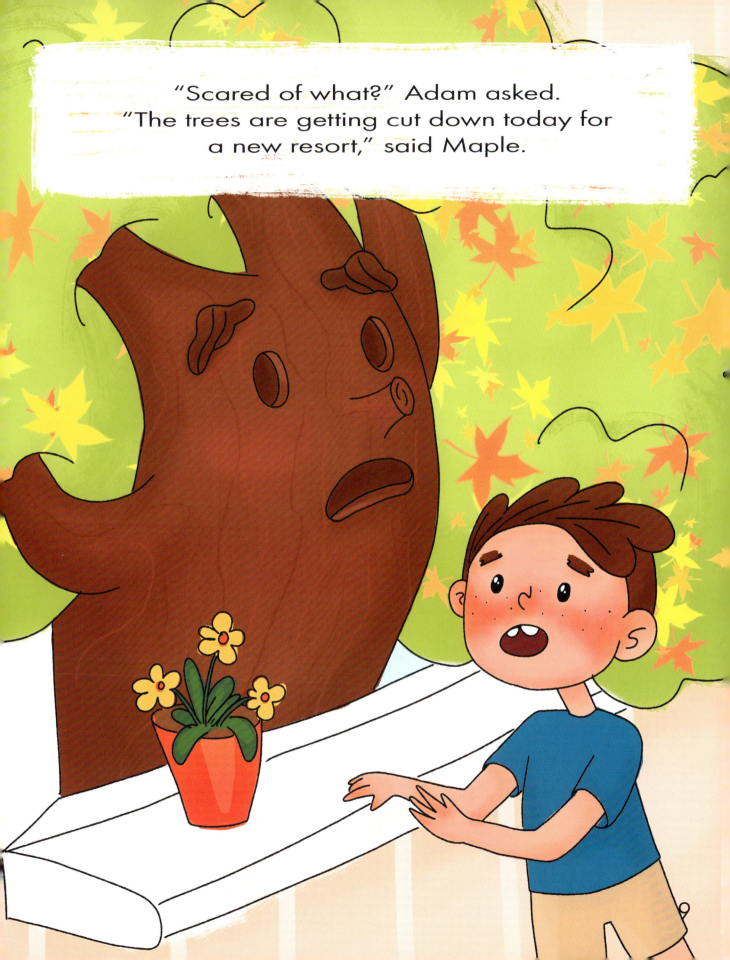

"Scared of what?" Adam asked.
"The trees are getting cut down today for a new resort," said Maple.

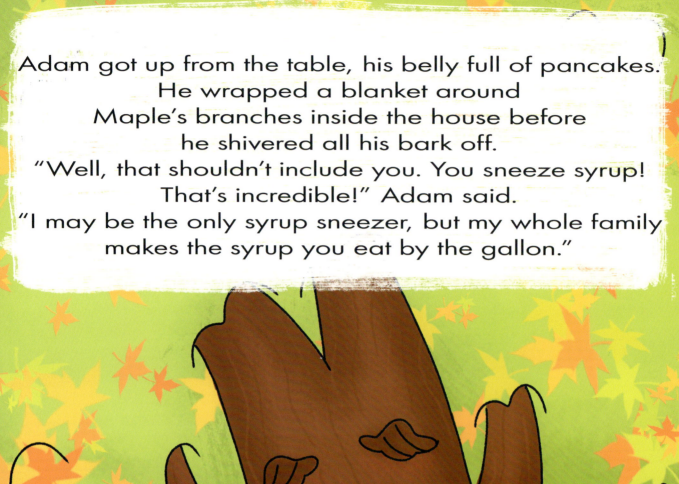

Adam got up from the table, his belly full of pancakes. He wrapped a blanket around Maple's branches inside the house before he shivered all his bark off.
"Well, that shouldn't include you. You sneeze syrup! That's incredible!" Adam said.
"I may be the only syrup sneezer, but my whole family makes the syrup you eat by the gallon."

Adam raked Maple's fallen leaves outside, thinking of a solution.
He decided to visit the construction crew and see if he could change some minds.

The machines were so loud.
"Excuse me. EXCUSE ME!" yelled Adam.
"Kid, get out of the way. We've got trees to cut," one of the construction workers yelled back.
"You can't cut down these trees! They're all special. More special than a new resort," Adam pleaded.

"Look, kid, I don't make the rules. All these trees are coming down today, and that's that. They're just trees."
"They're not just trees. They're great for climbing, building forts. . . and syrup!" said Adam. Back home, Adam found Maple in a puddle of syrup.

"Looks like it's up to us to stop this," Adam said to Maple.

Adam grabbed paper and markers to draw his sticky master plan with Maple.
"The construction begins here, and we are here. I'll get the garden hose, and we can put it up to your nose. Then you can sneeze syrup across the forest onto the machines."
"I like it! But what about—" Maple asked.
"What about what?" Adam asked.
"Since we're going to save the trees like heroes, we need to dress like heroes!" Maple exclaimed.

"Much better," Maple said.
"But what's that on your chest?"
"They're syrup balloons to throw at them!"
VAROOOOOOM!
CHUGGA CHUGGA CHUGGA!
"Maple, it's now or never."
Adam climbed up Maple's branches.

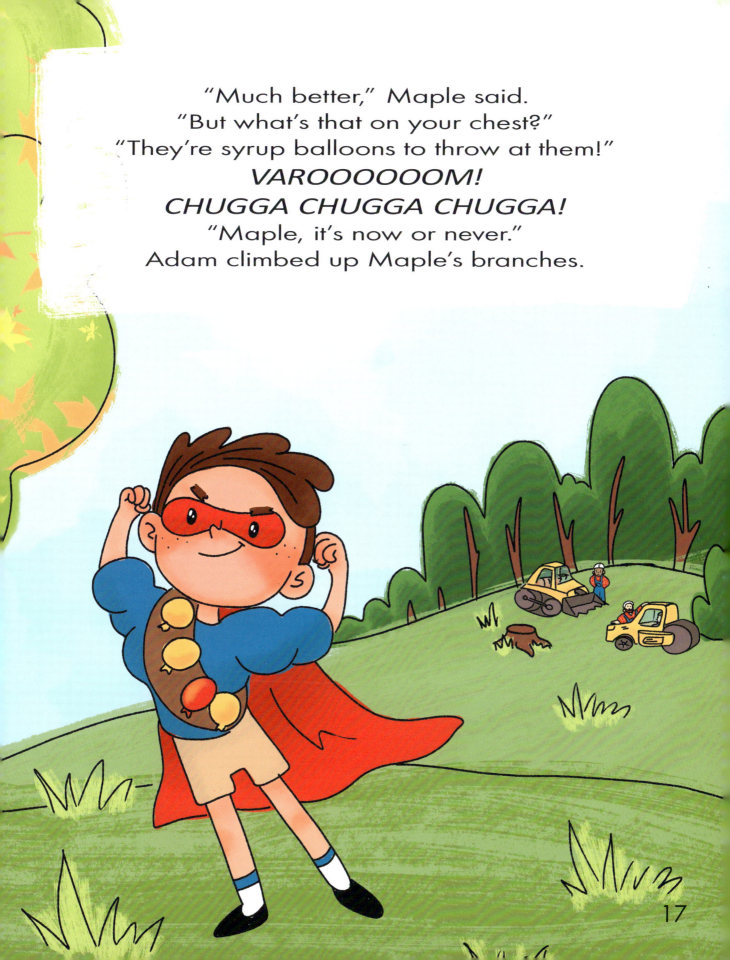

"Pass the hose... FIRE!"
Maple blew out the grossest, nastiest sneeze, and it shot through the hose, flying across the forest.
"Hit!" Maple yelled.
"It's not enough! Look!"
The machines were breaking down, but the construction workers grabbed their chainsaws and moved toward the trees.

"Maple, quick! Hold your branches out!"
Adam placed the balloons in Maple's branches.
"LAUNCH!"
"Hit!" Adam exclaimed.

"Hang on—why do they look happy?"

"This is tasty! I can only imagine this syrup drenched over pancakes!" said a construction worker with a huge smile.

"Maple, I have an idea," Adam said. Adam quickly ran home, grabbed some uneaten pancakes, and brought them to Maple.

"Let's take them over to the construction workers!" Adam said.

"What you all need are some pancakes to go with that delicious syrup my friend made."
"Just what I wanted! Hold on, who's your friend that made this syrup?" a construction worker asked.
"It's Maple! He's that tree over there. Look, if you cut these trees down, there won't be any more delicious syrup or trees to climb.
Trees are much more fun than a resort," said Adam.

"Instead of cutting the trees down, what would your boss think about a resort fort?" Adam asked.
"A resort FORT?"

The chainsaws dropped to the ground. Construction on the new resort fort began, with Adam and Maple's help, too!

As Adam and Maple celebrated,
he noticed something.
"Maple, you're not standing in a puddle of syrup anymore. . . or even shivering your bark off!"

"It's because I'm not scared anymore. My roots are here to stay."

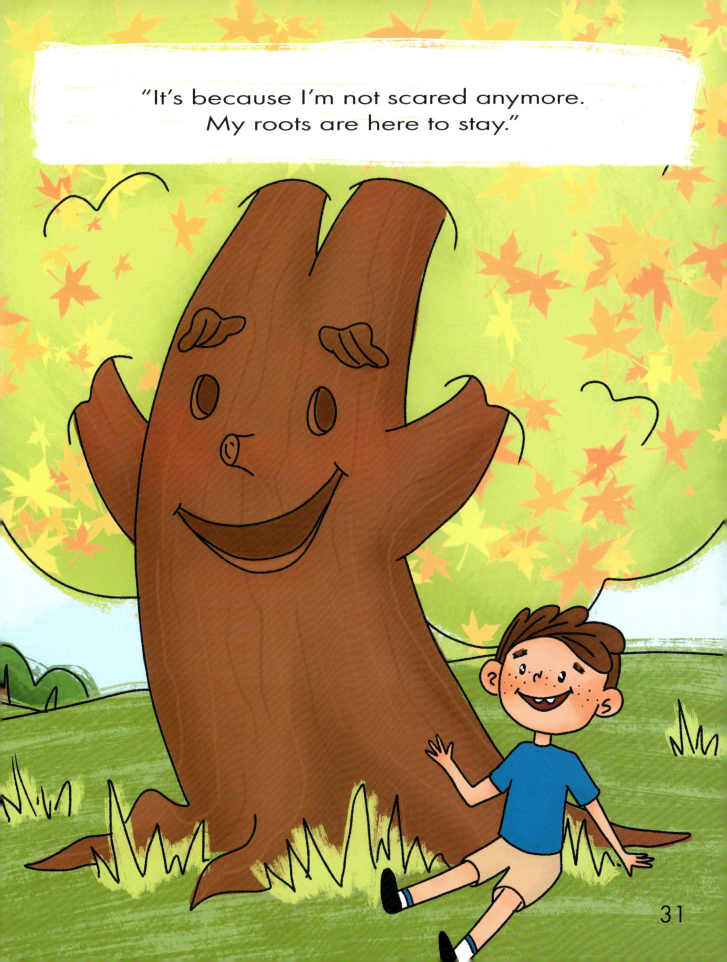